CW00502030

The Millionaire Monarch Metamorphosis Factor

A Transformational Leader's Intentional Journal Prompts Planner for Evolving & Launching From Your Millionaire Cocoon

AliNICOLE WOW!

The Millionaire Monarch Metamorphosis Factor

anwempires@gmail.com

ISBN-9798483217176

Printed in the United States of America by Kindle Direct Publishing

The Millionaire Monarch Metamorphosis Factor

You Are a Millionaire Monarch Transformational Leader

There is a unique millionaire experience encoding within Transformational Monarch Leaders for achieving greater levels of impact and income to support their life's mission and leadership movement.

Notice, I said a unique millionaire experience encoding. There's a difference between being a millionaire and having a millionaire experience.
The reason for this distinction is because the primary focus should be on aligning with your best life path and take notice of the millions that are already before you in your experience.

This can be in the areas of health, good relationships or even being able to purchase things at a certain price that would normally cost you an arm and leg or even cause you to spend money that you don't have. When you create a millionaire experience that type of lifestyle will open up to you and yes,

The Millionaire Monarch Metamorphosis Factor

indeed, you can certainly achieve becoming a millionaire in the process but first let's align with the experience and discover what this means for you.

This is all about transforming and evolving into the best version of yourself as a Monarch Leader as you extract your encoding to launch your life and leadership anew from your millionaire cocoon. You want to explore the evolution of who you have become versus the journey that you've evolved from.

The journey is not the butterfly. The butterfly is the evolution of your metamorphosis. This process has produced a new creation and the best-version of you for that phase. As you plan your next level, you will discover your encoding extraction factor by using the intentional journal prompts provided for three core areas of focus which are...

Transforming You & Evolving Into Your Best-Self

Creating a Millionaire Monarch Experience

Relaunching Your Life & Leadership Anew

Rinse and repeat this process at least three times.

The Millionaire Monarch Metamorphosis Factor

The Millionaire Monarch
Transformational Leader's
Evolutionary Encoding Extraction
Factor
Journal Prompts & Planner Section

The Millionaire Monarch Metamorphosis
Factor

Transforming You & Evolving Into Your Best-Self

Reverse engineer your evolution and be present with the vibration on completion for this phase.

The transformed best version of me at this phase looks like...

The Millionaire Monarch Metamorphosis Factor

Transforming You & Evolving Into Your Best-Self

Continued...

The Millionaire Monarch Metamorphosis Factor

Transforming You & Evolving Into Your Best-Self

My evolutionary outcome that produced this millionaire monarch experience was...

Creating a Millionaire Monarch Experience

Who Am I As A Millionaire?

The Millionaire Monarch Metamorphosis Factor

Creating a Millionaire Monarch Experience

As a millionaire I'm...

The Millionaire Monarch Metamorphosis Factor

Creating a Millionaire Monarch Experience

The millionaire experience I intended to create was...

The Millionaire Monarch Metamorphosis Factor

Creating a Millionaire Monarch Experience

My millionaire life and leadership looks like...

The Millionaire Monarch Metamorphosis Factor

Creating a Millionaire Monarch Experience

Who did I have to become in order to successfully evolve, achieve and sustain this new millionaire monarch experience?

The Millionaire Monarch Metamorphosis Factor

Creating a Millionaire Monarch Experience Continued...

The Millionaire Monarch Metamorphosis Factor

Relaunching Your Life & Leadership Anew

My millionaire monarch life and leadership cocoon launch experience game plan was...

The Millionaire Monarch Metamorphosis Factor

Relaunching Your Life & Leadership Anew

Continued...

The Millionaire Monarch Metamorphosis Factor

The Millionaire Monarch Metamorphosis
Factor

The Millionaire Monarch Metamorphosis
Factor

The Millionaire Monarch Metamorphosis
Factor

The Millionaire Monarch Metamorphosis
Factor

The Millionaire Monarch
Transformational Leader's
Evolutionary Encoding Extraction
Factor
Journal Prompts & Planner Section
Rinse & Repeat

The Millionaire Monarch Metamorphosis
Factor

Transforming You & Evolving Into Your Best-Self

Reverse engineer your evolution and be present with the vibration on completion for this phase.

The transformed best version of me at this phase looks like...

Transforming You & Evolving Into Your Best-Self

Continued...

Transforming You & Evolving Into Your Best-Self

My evolutionary outcome that produced this millionaire monarch experience was...

The Millionaire Monarch Metamorphosis Factor

Creating a Millionaire Monarch Experience

Who Am I As A Millionaire?

The Millionaire Monarch Metamorphosis Factor

Creating a Millionaire Monarch Experience

As a millionaire I'm...

The Millionaire Monarch Metamorphosis Factor

Creating a Millionaire Monarch Experience

The millionaire experience I intended to create was...

Creating a Millionaire Monarch Experience

My millionaire life and leadership looks like...

Creating a Millionaire Monarch Experience

Who did I have to become in order to successfully evolve, achieve and sustain this new millionaire monarch experience?

The Millionaire Monarch Metamorphosis Factor

Creating a Millionaire Monarch Experience Continued...

The Millionaire Monarch Metamorphosis Factor

Relaunching Your Life & Leadership Anew

My millionaire monarch life and leadership cocoon launch experience game plan was...

The Millionaire Monarch Metamorphosis Factor

Relaunching Your Life & Leadership Anew Continued...

The Millionaire Monarch Metamorphosis Factor

Continued Life & Leadership Planning

The Millionaire Monarch Metamorphosis
Factor

Continued Life & Leadership Planning

The Millionaire Monarch Metamorphosis
Factor

Continued Life & Leadership Planning

The Millionaire Monarch Metamorphosis
Factor

.

Continued Life & Leadership Planning

The Millionaire Monarch Metamorphosis Factor

The Millionaire Monarch Metamorphosis
Factor

The Millionaire Monarch
Transformational Leader's
Evolutionary Encoding Extraction
Factor
Journal Prompts & Planner Section
Rinse & Repeat

The Millionaire Monarch Metamorphosis
Factor

Transforming You & Evolving
Into Your Best-Self

Reverse engineer your evolution and be present with the vibration on completion for this phase.

The transformed best version of me at this phase looks like...

The Millionaire Monarch Metamorphosis Factor

Transforming You & Evolving Into Your Best-Self

Continued...

The Millionaire Monarch Metamorphosis Factor

Transforming You & Evolving Into Your Best-Self

My evolutionary outcome that produced this millionaire monarch experience was...

Creating a Millionaire Monarch Experience

Who Am I As A Millionaire?

The Millionaire Monarch Metamorphosis
Factor

Creating a Millionaire Monarch Experience

As a millionaire I'm...

The Millionaire Monarch Metamorphosis Factor

Creating a Millionaire Monarch Experience

The millionaire experience I intended to create was...

The Millionaire Monarch Metamorphosis Factor

Creating a Millionaire Monarch Experience

My millionaire life and leadership looks like...

The Millionaire Monarch Metamorphosis Factor

Creating a Millionaire Monarch Experience

Who did I have to become in order to successfully evolve, achieve and sustain this new millionaire monarch experience?

The Millionaire Monarch Metamorphosis Factor

Creating a Millionaire Monarch Experience Continued...

The Millionaire Monarch Metamorphosis Factor

Relaunching Your Life & Leadership Anew

My millionaire monarch life and leadership cocoon launch experience game plan was...

The Millionaire Monarch Metamorphosis Factor

Relaunching Your Life & Leadership Anew Continued...

The Millionaire Monarch Metamorphosis Factor

The Millionaire Monarch Metamorphosis
Factor

The Millionaire Monarch Metamorphosis
Factor

The Millionaire Monarch Metamorphosis
Factor

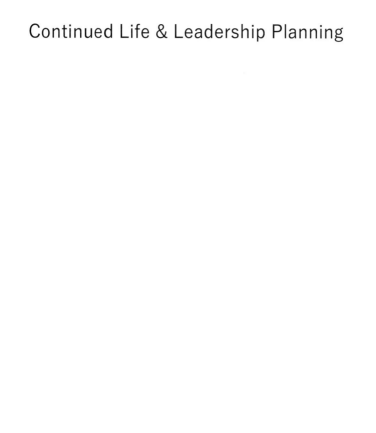

The Millionaire Monarch Metamorphosis
Factor

Continued Life & Leadership Planning

The Millionaire Monarch Metamorphosis
Factor

The Millionaire Monarch Metamorphosis
Factor

The Millionaire Monarch Metamorphosis
Factor

Continued Life & Leadership Planning

The Millionaire Monarch Metamorphosis
Factor

The Millionaire Monarch Metamorphosis
Factor

The Millionaire Monarch Metamorphosis
Factor

The Millionaire Monarch Metamorphosis
Factor

The Millionaire Monarch Metamorphosis
Factor

Continued Life & Leadership Planning

The Millionaire Monarch Metamorphosis Factor

Continued Life & Leadership Planning

The Millionaire Monarch Metamorphosis
Factor

Continued Life & Leadership Planning

The Millionaire Monarch Metamorphosis
Factor

For More Resources

Visit...

www.millionairepreneursmetamorphosis.tumblr.com

www.millionairemonarchleaderpreneurs.tumblr.com

To Book Author for Speaking, email...

www.wowshedoesitall@gmail.com

Learn more about the author at...

www.alinicolewow.com

If you found this resource helpful, please leave a positive review on Amazon.

Thanks & Many Blessings

The Millionaire Monarch Metamorphosis Factor

Printed in Great Britain
by Amazon

68441313R00043